Who Pooped in the Park?

Written by Gary D. Robson

Illustrated by Robert Rath

FARCOUNTRY
PRESS

HELENA, MONTANA

To the park rangers and interpretive staff
who have been a huge help to me in writing
the "Who Pooped" series.
- Gary

For Lucy and Thomas, my poop experts.
- Robert

ISBN 10: 1-56037-388-1
ISBN 13: 978-1-56037-388-9

© 2006 Farcountry Press
Text © 2006 Gary D. Robson
Illustrations © 2006 Farcountry Press

2006008415

For more information on our books,
write Farcountry Press, P.O. Box 5630, Helena, MT 59604;
call (800) 821-3874; or visit www.farcountrypress.com.

Library of Congress Cataloging-in-Publication Data

Robson, Gary D.
  Who pooped in the park?. Big Bend National Park / written by Gary D. Robson ; illustrated by Robert Rath.
    p. cm.
  ISBN-13: 978-1-56037-388-9
  ISBN-10: 1-56037-388-1
  1. Animal tracks--Texas--Big Bend National Park--Juvenile literature. I. Rath, Robert, ill. II. Title.
  QL768.R616 2006
  591.9764'932--dc22

Created, produced, and designed in the United States.
Printed in China.

11 10 09 08 07 06   1 2 3 4 5 6 7

"Dad? I have to go to the bathroom," said Michael as he squirmed in the back seat.

"We'll be at the campground soon," said Dad. "We're in Big Bend National Park now."

"He's just nervous," said Michael's sister. "He thinks a bear's gonna eat him." She growled at Michael and made her fingers look like claws.

"Stop it, Emily," said Mom. "Nobody is getting eaten by anything."

Michael was very excited about the trip, but Emily was right. He *was* nervous.

He was reading a book about grizzly bears. Michael knew how big they could get, and he was afraid that a hungry bear would eat just about anything—maybe even a boy.

"I *am* kind of scared of grizzly bears," Michael admitted.

"Don't worry," Dad told him. "There aren't any grizzlies in Big Bend National Park—or anywhere in Texas. Just black bears."

Mom reached back and held Michael's hand. She said, "We'll show you how to count a black bear's toes and never get close enough to be scared."

When they arrived at the campsite, Mom said, "Let's set up the tent. Then we can go for a walk and we'll show you what we mean."

Michael was worried about bear toes, but tried not to show it.

the STRAIGHT POOP

Big Bend National Park covers 800,000 acres—it's almost as big as the whole state of Rhode Island!

BIG BEND NATIONAL PARK

RHODE ISLAND

Emily looked around and said, "Look at those mountains! I thought Big Bend was a desert."

"Big Bend National Park is very big," Dad answered. "It has mountains, rivers, forests, and desert valleys, too. I've got the tent set up, and packed plenty of water, so we're ready."

"Hold still, Michael!" Mom said. "Even great explorers need sunscreen."

"Let's go!" said Emily. "I want to see some animals!"

Emily started to complain before they got very far. "Where are all the animals? I haven't seen any yet!"

the STRAIGHT POOP

Armadillos are the official state small mammal of Texas, but none live in Big Bend National Park.

"The animals are here," said Dad. "We just need to look for their *sign*."

"Sign?" said Michael. "Like a sign at a zoo?"

GREAT HORNED OWL

MULE DEER

RINGTAIL

Dad smiled. "In this case, a sign is a clue that an animal left behind. Look under that mesquite bush. An animal has been nibbling on the grass."

"All of these signs tell a story," added Mom. "See the little tracks the animal left in the dirt? You can count four toes in each footprint."

"Look over here! I found bunny poop, just like in Velvet's cage back home," yelled Michael.

"We came all the way to Big Bend National Park for *rabbit poop*?" Emily moaned. "Michael's bunny makes plenty of poop at home."

"Scientists and rangers call it *scat* instead of *poop*, kids," Mom said with a grin. "But you're right. This is from a rabbit or a hare."

the STRAIGHT POOP

Despite the name, jackrabbits aren't really rabbits—they're hares. They have longer legs and longer ears than rabbits. Black-tailed jackrabbits can leap up to 10 feet in one bound!

"See, Michael? We don't have to get up close to an animal to learn about it," said Dad. "Instead of a close encounter of the *scary* kind, we'll have a close encounter of the *poopy* kind!"

Everybody laughed, and Mom made a gross-out face.

13

"Here's some bigger bunny poop over here—I mean *rabbit scat*," said Michael, trying to sound grown up.

Mom took a look. "That's not from a rabbit," she said. "It's from a deer. The pellets are shaped like jellybeans, not round like rabbit scat."

DEER SCAT

JACKRABBIT SCAT

JELLYBEANS

the STRAIGHT POOP

Rabbits eat their own scat! They do this to get as much nutrition from their food as they can. The little brown balls are scat that's already been through twice.

"If that's deer scat, then are these deer footprints?" asked Emily. She was starting to have fun finding the clues the animals left behind.

"Yes," said Dad. "You can see how their hooves are split down the middle."

Michael spotted something on the ground. "Oh, no!" he said.
"Here's one of its antlers! Did the deer get eaten by a bear?"

Mom bent down by the antler. "Don't worry, the deer is
fine. This is called a 'shed' antler. The antlers fall off
every winter, and the deer grows a new,
bigger set the next year.

the STRAIGHT POOP

Female deer don't grow antlers, except for reindeer. They are the only type of deer in which the males and females both have antlers.

the STRAIGHT POOP

Horns are different than antlers. Antlers are shaped like branches and fall off every year. Horns never fall off and keep growing for the animal's entire life. Deer have antlers. Bighorn sheep have horns.

ANTLERS
ARE FORKED

ANTLERS HAVE POINTS
GROWING OFF ONE
MAIN "BEAM"

BIG EARS,
LIKE A
MULE

SMALLER
EARS

SKINNY TAIL
WITH BLACK TIP

FLUFFY TAIL, WHITE
ON THE BOTTOM
AND TAN ON TOP

MULE DEER

WHITE-TAILED DEER

"This antler is from a mule deer," said Dad.

"You can tell mule deer and white-tailed deer apart by the mule deer's forked antlers, big ears, and little tail with a black tip."

"This deer was in a hurry, though,"
said Mom as she studied the ground.

Emily and Michael went over to look.

"How can you tell?" said Emily.

"The hoofprints get very far apart here," explained Mom, "and the front prints are behind the back prints."

"The deer was walking backward?" said Michael.

"No, it was galloping. When deer run very fast, their tracks look much different than when they walk. Something must have scared this one!"

GALLOPING

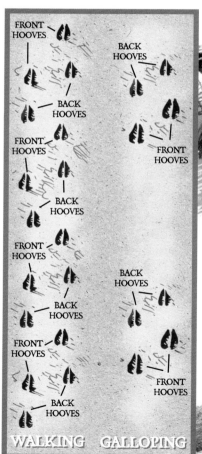

FRONT HOOVES
BACK HOOVES
BACK HOOVES
FRONT HOOVES
BACK HOOVES
FRONT HOOVES
BACK HOOVES
BACK HOOVES
FRONT HOOVES
BACK HOOVES
FRONT HOOVES
BACK HOOVES
FRONT HOOVES
BACK HOOVES

WALKING   GALLOPING

"Here's what scared the deer," Dad said. "There are coyote tracks and scat all around."

"Some of the tracks are small, like they're from pups," said Mom. "I'll bet their den is near here."

the STRAIGHT POOP

Coyotes eat just about anything they can catch, and they steal leftovers from other predators, too.

"The tracks look like dog tracks," said Michael.

"That's because the coyote is a member of the dog family," explained Dad.

the STRAIGHT POOP

If you look closely, you can tell coyote scat from dog scat. Coyotes eat small animals instead of dog food, so you'll find hair and bits of bone in the coyote scat.

"These look kind of like deer tracks," said Emily, "but they're smaller and not as pointy."

"The scat is different, too," added Michael. "Who pooped here?"

"That skunk smell is a clue," said Dad.

"But, Dad! Skunks don't have hooves!" said Emily.

"It wasn't a skunk," said Mom. "These tracks are from a collared peccary."

"That's a funny name," Emily giggled. "What's a peccary?"

"They're kind of like wild pigs," answered Dad. "Remember, they are wild animals, so don't get close."

the STRAIGHT POOP

Peccaries have a "musk gland" that makes them smell a little like a skunk. The smell is not normally very strong, but they get smellier when they are scared.

the STRAIGHT POOP

Many people in Texas call the collared peccary a javelina (pronounced have-a-LEE-na), which is the Spanish name for it.

23

"Is this another coyote track?" asked Emily. "It looks bigger."

"It also doesn't show any claw marks, and the front of the big pad looks dented in," said Mom. "Those are two clues that this is a cat track."

the STRAIGHT POOP

Cats can retract their claws, so their tracks don't normally show claw marks.

the STRAIGHT POOP

Because mountain lions eat other animals, you'll find hair and bits of bone in their scat.

"And since it's too big to be a bobcat track, it must be from a cougar," added Dad.

Michael had forgotten about bears but was getting a little worried about giant cats. "Are cougars as big as mountain lions?" he asked.

"Cougars and mountain lions are the same animal," replied Mom. "They're also called panthers, painters, pumas, and catamounts. That's a cat with a lot of names!"

COYOTE TRACKS

CLAW MARKS

LEADING TOE

DENT

MOUNTAIN LION TRACKS

DENT

LEADING TOE

the **STRAIGHT POOP**

C at tracks show a "leading toe." It sticks out a little bit farther than the other toes. Dog tracks do not have a leading toe—the front toes are more even.

"So no claw marks means the tracks are from a cat?" asked Emily.

"Most of the time. But there's one member of the dog family that has very small, sharp claws, so they don't usually show in their tracks," Mom answered.

"The gray fox," said Dad. "Gray foxes can even climb trees like cats! And because they like to sit up high and mark their territory with their scat, you can sometimes find fox scat in trees and up on top of big rocks!"

"Ow!" Emily sucked on her finger and frowned at a big plant. "This thing has sharp leaves!"

"That's a century plant," said Mom. "It only blooms once in its whole life, after it's 20 to 50 years old."

"People used to think they bloomed every 100 years. That's why they're called *century* plants," added Dad.

the STRAIGHT POOP

Apache Indians pulled the fibers out of the leaves of century plants and twisted them together to make ropes, sandals, and mats. They roasted and ate the center, or heart, of the plant.

"These are funny-looking tracks," said Michael, "and it looks like the dirt is all pushed around, too."

Mom went over to look. "Those tracks are from a roadrunner, Michael. And the swirls in the dirt show that it was chasing a fast-moving snake."

"Roadrunners eat *snakes*?" said Emily.

"They eat all kinds of animals," answered Dad. "Snakes, scorpions, lizards, mice, and even other birds."

the STRAIGHT POOP

Roadrunners can run up to 15 miles per hour! They don't fly very often or very far – maybe just into a tree to get away from a hungry coyote!

"Are these tracks
from a roadrunner, too?"
asked Michael.

"Let's see," said Dad. "The toes are wider,
and the backward-pointing toes aren't as
long. These must be from an owl!"

31

"But the best clues are these owl pellets on the ground," said Mom.

"Owl pellets?" said Emily.

"Owls eat their prey whole," explained Dad. "The parts they can't digest, like hair and bones, get coughed up in a pellet like this."

"Yuck!" said the kids.

"What kind of owl made the tracks and the cough pellets?" Michael asked.

"The bigger the tracks and the pellets, the bigger the owl," said Dad, "so it could be a great horned owl."

"Here's some really big scat," said Michael. "Who pooped here?"

"I know who!" Emily said excitedly. "A horse!"

the STRAIGHT POOP

Horses can walk while they poop, but they stop and stand still to pee.

34

"Right," said Mom. "And here are some hoofprints from the horse, too."

"Those are funny-looking hoofprints," said Michael.

"Horses don't have split hooves like deer and peccaries," said Dad. "Each hoof has just one part."

"I think he's talking about the horseshoes," said Mom. "They make the hoofprints look different."

the STRAIGHT POOP

Horses that are ridden a lot have metal shoes attached to their hooves to protect them from wear. Horse tracks show the shape of the horseshoe.

DEER TRACKS

HORSE TRACKS

HORSE TRACKS WITH HORSESHOE

"These tracks are weird, too," said Michael. "It looks like the coyote track, but way smaller."

"And there are more toes and an extra pad in the back," said Dad. "It's a ringtail track."

Emily's eyes lit up. "Ringtails are cool! I love those big eyes. Do you think we'll see one?"

the STRAIGHT POOP

Ringtails eat other small animals, birds, insects, and plants.

"Ringtails are nocturnal, which means they sleep during the day and come out at night," replied Mom. "So we probably won't see one."

39

"What happened to this tree?" asked Michael.

"Something was sharpening its claws, Michael, and if you look how high those scratch marks go, it was pretty big," said Mom.

40

"It's not just the animal that's big," said Emily. "Look at the size of this poop!"

"It looks like we found Michael's black bear," said Dad.

Michael jumped. "Where?" he asked.

the STRAIGHT POOP

Black bears eat almost anything. They mostly live on leaves, nuts, berries, insects, twigs, and honey, but they also eat carrion (dead animals) and hunt small animals.

"I mean we found its scat," said Dad. "Let's see what you learned today. What can you figure out about this bear?"

"The bear's as tall as Dad, and it has really long claws," said Michael, looking at the scratch marks on the tree.

"It's been eating plants," said Emily, "because there's no hair or bones in this poop."

"Good!" Mom said. "What else?"

"Here's its footprint," said Michael. "The track is really big, and it has five toes like a ringtail instead of four like a mountain lion."

"I told you you'd be able to count a black bear's toes," laughed Mom.

As they ate dinner that night, everyone talked about how much fun they had.

"We didn't see very many animals," said Emily, "but it seemed like we did!"

Everyone laughed when Michael said, "And I didn't get scared once!"

TRACKS and

BLACK BEAR

FRONT

BACK

Five toes on each foot. Large tracks with visible claws.

Scat changes depending on diet but usually contains plant parts.

MOUNTAIN LION

LEADING TOE

DENT

LEFT FRONT

RIGHT BACK

Four toes on each foot. Tracks are bigger than a coyote's, but claw marks don't show. Note dent in pad of front tracks and leading toes.

Scat is larger than coyote scat. It is rounded, with fur and bone in it.

COYOTE

FRONT

BACK

Four toes on each foot. Tracks look like dog tracks and usually show claw marks.

Scat is very dark colored with tapered ends and usually contains hair.

GRAY FOX

FRONT

BACK

Four toes on each foot. Tracks are smaller than a coyote's, with a ridge on the large pad.

Scat is similar to coyote scat, but often contains plant and insect parts.

GREAT HORNED OWL

Tracks show four toes: two pointing forward and two back or sideways.

Scat is runny and white. "Cough pellets" contain fur and bones.

SCAT NOTES

BLACK-TAILED JACKRABBIT

FRONT

BACK

Four toes on each foot. Small tracks are filled in between the toes.

The scat is in little brown balls.

DEER

FRONT

BACK

Each track is pointy and split into two parts.

Scat is oval-shaped like jellybeans, not round like rabbit scat.

COLLARED PECCARY OR JAVELINA

FRONT

FRONT

BACK

Each track is split into two parts like deer but is not as pointy. They also show a shorter stride than a deer.

Scat is usually in large, uneven chunks.

HORSE

FRONT

BACK

Tracks are much bigger than deer or peccary tracks and are not split into two parts.

Scat is in chunks, with plant parts often visible.

RINGTAIL

FRONT

BACK

Five toes on each foot. Claws do not usually show.

Scat crumbles easily and often has insect parts in it.

ABOUT the AUTHOR and ILLUSTRATOR

GARY ROBSON owns a bookstore in Red Lodge, Montana, and lives on a ranch near Yellowstone National Park. He has written on a wide variety of subjects for both children and adults and taught at several colleges in Montana and California. He is an expert on closed captioning technology for deaf and hard-of-hearing people.

www.whopooped.com

ROBERT RATH

is a book designer and illustrator living in Bozeman, Montana. Although he has worked with Scholastic Books, Lucasfilm, and Montana State University, his favorite project is keeping up with his family.

www.robertrath.net

Who Pooped in the Park?™

OTHER BOOKS IN THE WHO POOPED IN THE PARK?™ SERIES:

Acadia National Park

Black Hills

Death Valley National Park

Glacier National Park

Grand Canyon National Park

Grand Teton National Park

Great Smoky Mountains National Park

Olympic National Park

Red Rock Canyon National Conservation Area

Rocky Mountain National Park

Sequoia/Kings Canyon National Parks

Shenandoah National Park

Sonoran Desert

Yellowstone National Park

Yosemite National Park